811.   15253

             Moore, Lilian $9.95

            Something new begins

DATE			

Imperial Public Library
Imperial, Texas

© THE BAKER & TAYLOR CO

BOOKS BY LILIAN MOORE

Papa Albert
I Feel the Same Way
I Thought I Heard the City
Sam's Place
See My Lovely Poison Ivy
To See the World Afresh
(*Compiled by Lilian Moore
and Judith Thurman*)
Think of Shadows
Something new begins...

Something new begins

Something new begins

by Lilian Moore

NEW AND SELECTED POEMS

Illustrated by Mary Jane Dunton

ATHENEUM 1982 NEW YORK

Wind Poem (Wind Song) and Dragon Smoke were originally
printed in the Lucky Book Club Memo to Teachers.
Copyright © 1966 by Scholastic Magazine, Inc.

Library of Congress Cataloging in Publication Data

Moore, Lilian.   Something new begins—.

Summary: Includes fifteen new poems, as well as poems
selected from six earlier collections.
1. Children's poetry, American. [1. American poetry]
I. Title.
PS3563.O622S6   811'.54   82-1723
ISBN 0-689-30818-3   AACR2

Poems copyright © 1967, 1969, 1972, 1975, 1980, 1982 by Lilian Moore
Graphics copyright © 1982 by Mary Jane Dunton
All rights reserved
Published simultaneously in Canada by McClelland & Stewart, Ltd.
Composition by American-Stratford Graphic Services, Brattleboro, Vt.
Printed and bound by Fairfield Graphics, Fairfield, Pennsylvania
Designed by Mary Jane Dunton
First Edition

Remembering with love

Aaron and Sarah Levenson

Contents

1 SOMETHING NEW BEGINS

Beach Stones	3
Sun on Rain	4
Fog Lifting	5
The Whale Ghost	6
Song of the Tree Frogs	8
While You Were Chasing a Hat	9
Winding Road	10
Stampede	12
Jetstream	13
Mural on Second Avenue	14
Lost	16
Corn Talk	18
Hurricane	20
Fossils	21
December 21	22

2 SELECTED POEMS

I THOUGHT I HEARD THE CITY

The Bridge	27
The Tree on the Corner	28
Night Snow	28
Snowy Morning	29
Pigeons	30
Construction	31
Forsythia Bush	32
Reflections	33
Foghorns	34
Rain Pools	34
To a Red Kite	35
Winter Dark	36
Summer Rain	37

3 SELECTED POEMS

LITTLE RACCOON AND POEMS FROM THE WOODS

Message From a Caterpillar	41
Move Over	42
Night Creature	43
Yellow Weed	44
New Sounds	45
Woodpecker	46
Odd	47
Spider	48
Rain	49

I FEEL THE SAME WAY

SELECTED POEMS

Until I Saw the Sea	53
Mine	54
Go Wind	55
Wind Song	56
True	57
Dragon Smoke	58
In the Fog	58
In the Sun	59

SEE MY LOVELY POISON IVY

SELECTED POEMS

The Witch's Song	63
The Troll Bridge	64
I Wish	65
I Left My Head	66
Look at That!	67
The Witch's Garden	68
Bedtime Story	69
Lost and Found	70

6 THINK OF SHADOWS

SELECTED POEMS

Crow Wonders	75
Partners	76
Fence	76
In the Park	77
Recess	78
Long Shadow Story	79
Cloud Shadow	80
Bike Ride	81
Telling Time	82
The First	83
Tree Shadows	84
Tonight	85

7 SAM'S PLACE

The Shawangunks—Early April	89
Encounter	90
Wet	91
Patriarchs	92
Green	93
Letter to a Friend	94
Dry Spell	96

Hay Song	97
Sun Day	98
Ecology	100
Sunset	101
Arson	102
The Chestnuts Are Falling	103
Squirrel	104
September	105
Recycled	106
Flight	108
Willow Yellow	109
Winter Cardinal	110
Weather Report	111

BEACH STONES

When these small
stones
were
in clear pools and
nets of weed

tide-tumbled
teased by spray

they glowed
moonsilver,
glinted sunsparks on
their speckled
skins.

Spilled on the
shelf
they were
wet-sand jewels
wave-green
still flecked with
foam.

Now
gray stones
lie
dry and dim.

Why did we bring them home?

SUN ON RAIN

The sun is out
and suddenly,
rain!

Sun on rain.

A million raindrops
shatter the
light

let loose
the captive
colors

spill streams of
violet, indigo
blue

scatter green fire
and yellow
glow

let fly
the orange, the
rampant red

and
set free a
rainbow.

FOG LIFTING

All day
    sea breath
fogged us in.

Now we see the
    horizon
distant, thin

and the sky bending
    down to say
here I begin
    or end

and the sea rolling
    out to say
here I end
    or begin.

THE WHALE GHOST

When we've emptied
the sea of the
last great
whale

will he come
rising
from a deep remembered
dive

sending from his
blowhole
a ghostly fog
of spout?

Will he call
with haunting cry

to his herd that
rode the
seas with joyous
ease,

to the whale that swam
beside him,

to the calf?

Will we hear his
sad song
echoing
over the water?

SONG OF THE TREE FROGS

Here come the
bagpipers
of the bog,
the peepers

filling the March winds
with a thin whistling
din

shrilling
from the ponds,
the wet rocks, the
low willows

the opening notes
of the
tree frog
chorus

the non-stop
skirl of sound.

It's spring
when the peepers
say so.

WHILE YOU WERE CHASING A HAT

The wind
that whirled
your hat
away

        furled a flag
        filled a sail

        raced a boat
        tugged a kite

        tweaked its tail

        towed a cloud
        rode a wave

        chased some crows
        flung them far

        strummed on a
        telephone wire
        guitar

        thrumming a tune
        mile on mile
        all the while you

were
chasing
  a hat.

WINDING ROAD

The road
winds and
winds

and
in a far field
a shadow-horse is
grazing.

A sudden turn —

a bright white house,
and a flop-eared dog is
lazing
on the porch
in the sun.

The road
winds

and now we see
the field is dense with
clover.
The horse
switches his tail,
moves over
to watch us
go by.

The house is
far now.
A tiny dog
sleeps there
in the sun.

The road
winds

and they are
gone,
the horse
the field of clover
the house
the dreaming dog.

STAMPEDE

Dark clouds
shove
and crowd

butting like old gray
goats

trampling
white fleece and
blue sky

the herd charging now,
surging,
rumbling —

Run!
Here comes the rain.

JETSTREAM

A jet screams and climbs

and in a glare
of
blue

a white trail streams across the sky

like the wake
of a
speedboat.

Come!
Ski a sky slope.
Ride a jet tail.

But

HURRY *hurry hurry*

MURAL ON SECOND AVENUE

Someone
stood here
tall on a ladder,
dreaming
to the slap of a
wet brush,

painting
on the blank
unwindowed wall of
this old house.

Now the wall is a
field of wild
grass,
bending to a wind.

A unicorn's grazing there
beside a
zebra.

A giraffe
is nibbling a
treetop

and in a sky of
eye-blinking
blue

a horse is flying.

All
right at home in the
neighborhood.

LOST

What happened in the sky
today?

Why did the
wild geese flying
south

turn north
in
disarray,

the whole flock
drifting?

Did clouds
blur the
sun

or mist
hide the
hills?

Did strange
winds
blow,

shifting the great
geese in their
flight?

Did they ever spy
the river's
glint

and find the way?

CORN TALK

Listen to a cornstalk
whispering
to the autumn wind,

> "Once I was a
> kernel, juicy in
> tight skin.
>
> Long long ago
> in April
> I sank into new-turned
> earth.
>
> In the warm sweet
> dark, I drank
> rain.
>
> Stretched by light
> I grew
> green-tall,

     prince of the garden
     in fringed tassels,
     in proud summer
     silks.

     Plump kernels
     fattened on my
     stalk,
     each ear secret,
     mummy-wrapped . . ."

"Corn talk again!"
sighs the wind
in the empty garden.

HURRICANE

All night
the wind
poured
through the trees,

roared
like a waterfall,
tugged and
tore.

In the morning light
the stunned
trees
looked down on

tattered leaves
heaped in
brown
hills

torn twigs
flung
in barbed wire
tangles

battered
branches
crossed like
swords.

FOSSILS

Older than
books,
than scrolls,

older
than the first
tales told

or the
first words
spoken

are the stories

in forests that
turned to
stone

in ice walls
that trapped the
mammoth

in the long
bones of
dinosaurs —

the fossil
stories that begin
Once upon a time

DECEMBER 21

Old Witch Winter,
is riding high,
this day of her longest
night.

"Ice!"
she shrieks.
No puddle is safe,
roofs bristle with
spears.

"Light
begone!"
she whistles.
Dusk appears.

"Shiver!"
she snarls.
We heed, and
huddle in our
skins.

Thermometers
bleed to
zero,

but something new
begins.

I THOUGHT I HEARD THE CITY

Selected Poems

THE BRIDGE

A bridge
by day
is steel and strong.
It carries
giant trucks that roll along
above the waters
of the bay.
A bridge is steel and might —
till night.

A bridge
at night
is spun of light
that someone tossed
across the bay
and someone caught
and pinned down tight —
till day.

THE TREE ON THE CORNER

I've seen
the tree on the corner
in spring bud
and summer green.
Yesterday
it was yellow gold.

Then a cold
wind began to blow.
Now I know —
you really do not see
a tree
until you see
its bones.

NIGHT SNOW

A ghostly snow
floats
out of the sky
tonight,
and snow moths
dance
in the pale street light.

SNOWY MORNING

Wake
gently this morning
to a different day.
Listen.

There is no bray
of buses,
no brake growls,
no siren howls and
no horns
blow.

There is only
the silence
of a city
hushed
by snow.

PIGEONS

Pigeons are city folk
content
to live with concrete
and cement.

They seldom
try
the sky.

A pigeon never sings
of hill
and flowering hedge,
but busily commutes
from sidewalk
to his ledge.

        Oh pigeon, what a waste of wings!

CONSTRUCTION

The giant mouth
chews
rocks
spews them
and is back for
more.

The giant arm
swings up
with a girder
for
the fourteenth floor.

Down there,
a tiny man
is
telling them
where
to put a skyscraper.

FORSYTHIA BUSH

There is nothing
quite
like the sudden
light

of
forsythia
that
one morning
without warning

explodes
into yellow
and
startles the street
into spring.

REFLECTIONS

On this street
of windowed stores
see,
in the glass
shadow people meet
and pass
and glide to
secret places.

Ghostly mothers
hold
the hands of dim gray children,
scold
them silently
and melt away.

And
now and then,
before
the window mirror
of a store,
phantom faces
stop
and window shop.

FOGHORNS

The foghorns moaned
    in the bay last night
  so sad
  so deep
I thought I heard the city
    crying in its sleep.

RAIN POOLS

The rain
litters
the street
with mirror splinters
silver,
brown.

Now
each piece
glitters with

sky
cloud
tree

upside down.

TO A RED KITE

Fling
yourself
upon the sky.

Take the string
you need.
Ride high

high
above the park.
Tug and buck
and lark
with the wind.

Touch a cloud,
red kite.
Follow the wild geese
in their flight.

WINTER DARK

Winter dark comes early
mixing afternoon
and night.
Soon
there's a comma of a moon,

and each streetlight
along the
way
puts its period
to the end of day.

Now
a neon sign
punctuates the dark
with a bright
blinking
breathless
exclamation mark!

SUMMER RAIN

The sky is
scrubbed
of every smudge of
cloud.

The sidewalk is a
slate
that's quickly
dry.

Light
dazzles
like
a washed
window pane,

and
I

breathe
the freshly laundered
air
of after-rain.

LITTLE RACCOON
AND POEMS FROM THE WOODS

Selected Poems

MESSAGE FROM A CATERPILLAR

Don't shake this
bough.
Don't try
to wake me
now.

In this cocoon
I've work to
do.
Inside this silk
I'm changing
things.

I'm worm-like now
but in this
dark
I'm growing
wings.

MOVE OVER

    Big
    burly
    bumblebee
    buzzing
    through the grass,
move over.

    Black and
    yellow
    clover rover,
let me pass.

    Fat and
    furry
    rumblebee
    loud on the
    wing,
    let me
    hurry
    past
your sting.

NIGHT CREATURE

I like
the quiet breathing
of the night,

the tree talk
the wind-swish
the star light.

Day is
glare-y
loud
scary.
Day bustles.

Night rustles.
I like
night.

YELLOW WEED

How did you get here,
weed?
Who brought your seed?

Did it lift
on the wind and
sail
and drift
from a far and yellow
field?

Was your seed a
burr,
a sticky burr that
clung to a
fox's
furry tail?

Did it fly with a
bird
who liked to feed
on the tasty
seed
of the yellow
weed?

How did you come?

NEW SOUNDS

New sounds to
walk on
today,

dry
leaves
talking
in hoarse
whispers
under bare trees.

WOODPECKER

Small sounds,
secret stirrings
under the
tree bark

drummmmmmm!
drillllll!
Woodpecker's
needle bill
drives
digs
dives into a
neat
new
hole . . .

Ah!
Grubworms.

ODD

That was
odd
I must
say.

As I sat
on the
stump,
a piece of road
took
a lively
jump.

A small brown
clod
leaped
up
and away.

A piece of road!

Well, it *might*
have been
a tiny
toad.

SPIDER

Spider's
spinning

Spider's
beginning

another web.

(Spin
 low)

Thinning her long
and silky
thread

(Spin
 high)

Spider's
spinning
her
silver lace.

Isn't her web
a lovely
place?

Ask fly.

RAIN

mud
puddled
paths

damp
robins
in splashed nests

flood
in the woodchuck's
burrow

wet fur
wet feather
weather

I FEEL THE SAME WAY

Selected Poems

UNTIL I SAW THE SEA

Until I saw the sea
I did not know
that wind
could wrinkle water so.

I never knew
that sun
could splinter a whole sea of blue.

Nor
did I know before,
a sea breathes in and out
upon a shore.

MINE

I made a sand castle.
In rolled the sea.
    "All sand castles
   belong to me,
     to me,"
said the sea.

I dug sand tunnels.
In flowed the sea.
    "All sand tunnels
   belong to me,
     to me,"
said the sea.

I saw my sand pail floating free.
I ran and snatched it from the sea.
    "My sand pail
   belongs to me —
to *me!*"

GO WIND

Go wind, blow
Push wind, swoosh.
      Shake things
      take things
      make   things
            fly.

      Ring things
      swing things
      fling things
          high.

Go wind, blow
Push things
wheee.
      No, wind, no.
      Not me —
      not *me*.

WIND SONG

When the wind blows
The quiet things speak.
Some whisper, some clang,
Some creak.

Grasses swish.
Treetops sigh.
Flags slap
and snap at the sky.
Wires on poles
whistle and hum.
Ashcans roll.
Windows drum.

When the wind goes,
suddenly
then,
the quiet things
are quiet again.

TRUE

When
the green eyes
of a cat
look deep into
you

you know
that
whatever it is
they are saying
is
true.

DRAGON SMOKE

Breathe and blow
white clouds
    with every puff.
It's cold today,
    cold enough
to see your breath.
Huff!
    Breathe dragon smoke
        today!

IN THE FOG

Stand still.
The fog wraps you up
and no one can find you.

Walk.
The fog opens up
to let you through
and closes behind you.

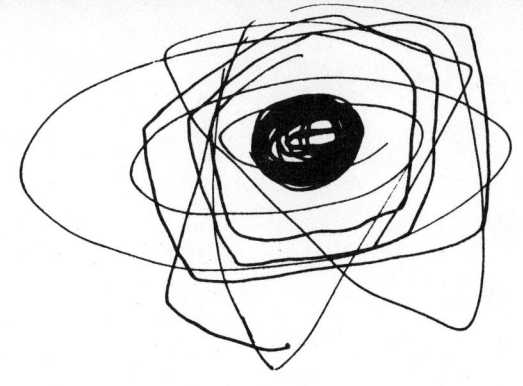

IN THE SUN

Sit
on your doorstep
or any place.

Sit
in the sun
and lift your face.

Close your eyes and
sun dream.
Soon the warm warm sun
will seem
to fill you up
and
spill over.

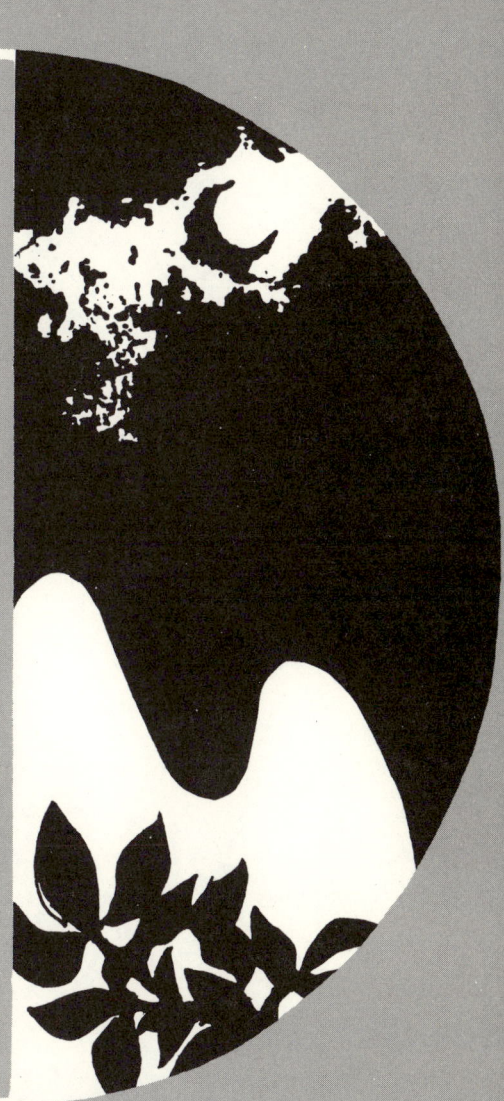

SEE MY LOVELY POISON IVY

Selected Poems

THE WITCH'S SONG

Hey! Cackle! Hey!
Let's have fun today.

> All shoelaces will have knots.
> No knots will untie.
> Every glass of milk will spill.
> Nothing wet will dry.
> Every pencil point will break.
> And everywhere in town
> Peanut-buttered bread will drop
> Upside down.

Hey! Hey! Hey!
Have a pleasant day.

THE TROLL BRIDGE

This is the Bridge
of the
Terrible Troll.
No one goes
by
without paying
a toll,
a terrible toll
to the Troll.

It's no place to
loll, to
linger or
stroll,
to sing or to
play.

So if ever you
ride
to the
opposite side,
be ready to
pay
the terrible troll
I mean terrible toll
to the Terrible Toll —
I mean Troll.

I WISH

"I wish,"
Said Baby Bat,
"That I could
Get
A Boy or Girl
To have me
For a pet.

We'd live
Inside this cold
Old cave
Safe from sunny weather,
Swooping out in
Darkest night
To feed on bugs
Together.

Then
Hanging in our
Cave we'd stay
Playing, upside down
All day!"

I LEFT MY HEAD

I left my head
somewhere
today.
Put it down for
just
a minute.
Under the
table?
On a chair?
Wish I were
able
to say
where.
Everything I need
is
in it!

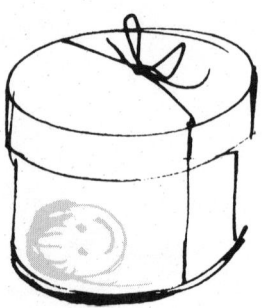

LOOK AT THAT!

Look at that!
Ghosts lined up
at the laundromat,
all around the
block.

Each has
bleach
and some
detergent.

Each one seems to
think it
urgent

to take a spin
in a
washing machine

before the
clock
strikes
Halloween!

THE WITCH'S GARDEN

In the witch's
garden
the gate is open
wide.

"Come inside,"
says the
witch.
"Dears,
come inside.

No flowers
in *my* garden,
nothing mint-y
nothing chive-y.

Come inside,
come inside.
See my lovely
poison ivy."

BEDTIME STORY

"Tell me a story,"
Says Witch's Child,

"About the Beast
So fierce and wild.

About a Ghost
That shrieks and groans,

A Skeleton
That rattles bones,

About a Monster
Crawly-creepy.

Something nice
To make me sleepy."

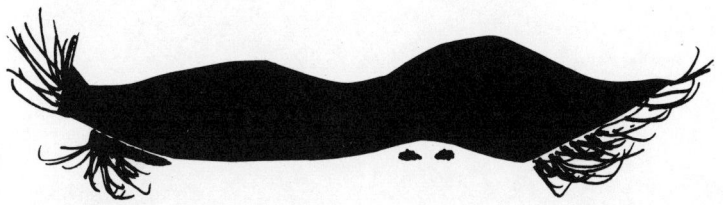

LOST AND FOUND

LOST:
A Wizard's loving pet.
Rather longish.
Somewhat scaly.
May be hungry or
upset.
Please feed daily.

P.S. Reward

FOUND:
A dragon
breathing fire.
Flails his scaly
tail
in ire.
Would eat twenty LARGE meals
daily
if we let him.
Please
Come and get him.

P.S. No reward necessary.

CROW WONDERS

Crow knows
that hat,
that baggy coat,
that raggy ruff at the throat.
Old stuff!

The straw man
hasn't fluttered
a hand,
muttered a sound,
and the corn is sweet.

But what's
that dark thing
at his feet,
growing longer,
longer
in
the
sun?

PARTNERS

This is the wind's doing,
this clothesline
dance,
>shirttails twirling,
>sleeves
>clapping, thigh-slapping,
>jeans stepping high.

This is the sun's doing,
these shadows
leaping, twisting,
prancing —
partners dancing
to the same tune.

FENCE

>White picket fence
>Boy with a stick:
>>*Whackety crackety*
>>*Clackety*
>>*Click*
>
>Shadow boy with a stick
>Shadow fence on the ground:
>>Shadow whack, shadow crack
>>Shadow clack.
>>Not a sound.

IN THE PARK

When you've
run races
in the sun,

stolen bases,
pumped high on a
swing,

when you've
jumped Double Dutch
too much,

played

till you're
sun drunk
sun dizzy —

how shivery cool
to fling
yourself
into the tree's great
pool
of
shade.

RECESS

The children
scribble their shadows
on the school yard,

scribble
scribble
on a great blackboard —

lanky leg
shadows
running into
lifted arm shadows
flinging
bouncing ball shapes
into skinny upside down shadows
swinging
on
long monkey bars

till
a cloud
moving
across the morning sun
wipes out all
scribbles
like a giant
eraser.

LONG SHADOW STORY

Giraffe's
shadow
moves off
in the morning light

glides over
brown brush, over
growing grass,
embraces a distant
tree

stretches its
longest-neck-in-the-world,

touches

shadows swooping,
slinking,
small shapes that
scurry

travels back,
no hurry,
settles down at
Giraffe's feet
in the high noon sun.

CLOUD SHADOW

A monster
sleeps
on a mountain.
Why?

        A monster
        cloud
        rests
        in the sky.

When the wind
blows,
and the cloud
drifts,

watch

        below,
        the monster
        shifts,

        lifts
        its heavy head,

        opens
        its great paws
        and slips away.

BIKE RIDE

Look at us!

We ride a
road
the sun has paved with
shadows.

We glide
on leaf lace
across tree spires
over
shadow ropes
of droopy wires.

We roll
through a shade tunnel
into light.

Look!
Our bikes
spin
black-and-white
shadow
pinwheels.

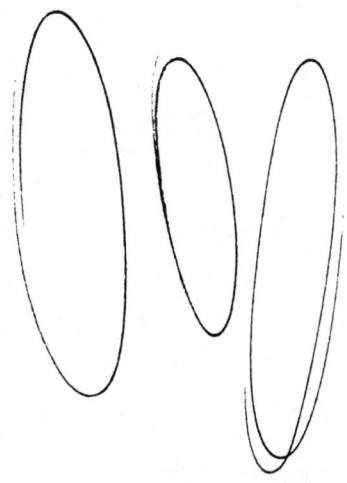

TELLING TIME

Time ticks,
whispers,
rings,
sounds a chime,
a ping,
a tock,
or the long slow
bong
of a grandfather clock.

Time
on the sundial
is a
shadow,
making its rounds,
moving
till day is done
in secret
understanding
with the sun.

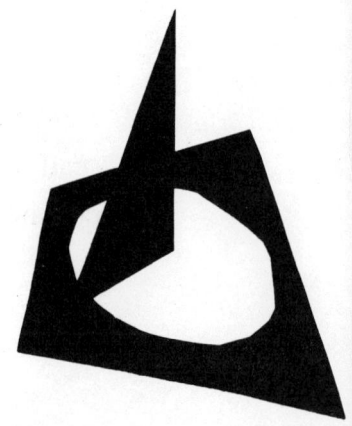

THE FIRST

Moon,
remember
how men left their
planet
in streams of
flame,
rode weightless
in the skies
till you pulled
them down,
and then
in the blinding sunlight
how the first shadow
of an
Earthling
lay
on your
bleak dust?

TREE SHADOWS

The shadow of a
tree
can be

a willow,
hair tossing
in the summer wind,

a gaunt oak in the
fall,
bereft
no leaf left,

can be

the pine in
moonlight,
black on the snow
like a
wing

or the shadow of
maples
not yet solid
in the spring.

TONIGHT

Strange shadows out
tonight
in the white
light
of the moon

shaggy humps
dark baggy bumps
meeting
darting

bat shapes
pointed heads
parting
greeting.

Strange shadows out
tonight,
all tricking and treating.

SAM'S PLACE

THE SHAWANGUNKS
— EARLY APRIL

Thin streams
wait
for slopes
to shed snow
skins.

Rock ledges
wear
ice beards
like
mandarins.

These
old hills
crouch
winterbound,
slow to yield
the season.

Now
spring winds
flowing northward
must
unclench
this ground.

ENCOUNTER

We both stood
heart-stopping
still,

I in the doorway
the deer
near
the old apple tree,

he
muscle wary
straining
to hear

I holding breath
to say
do not fear.

In the silence
between us
my thought said
stay!

Did it snap
like a twig?
He rose on a curve
and fled.

WET

Wet wet wet
the world of melting winter,
icicles weeping themselves away
on the eaves
little brown rivers streaming
down the road
nibbling
at the edges of the tired snow,
  all puddled mud
  not a dry place to put
  a booted foot,
everything
  dripping
  gushing
  slushing
  slipping
and listen to that brook,
rushing
like a puppy loosed from its leash.

PATRIARCHS

No one at Sam's place
remembers
when these apple trees
were young
and fruit hung
heavy
on the bough.

Now
they wear
their thinning blossoms
like white hair
and stand
dryboned

old
unbending
in the cold
and early winds
of spring.

". . . green is good for the eyes."
THE UGLY DUCKLING
BY HANS CHRISTIAN ANDERSEN

GREEN

Ducklings,
look around.

That's treegreen
filling the sky

and there's grassgreen
running
up the hill,
steeply.

The shadowgreen is
pine woods,
dark
old.

The yellowgreen is
young leaf
unfolding,
new
as you.

Breathe green
deeply.

LETTER TO A FRIEND

Come soon.

Everything is lusting
for light,
thrusting
up
up
splitting the earth,
opening flaring fading,
seed
into shoot
bud
into flower,
nothing
beyond its hour.

Come soon.

The apple bloom has melted
like
spring snow.

The lilac
changed the air,
surprising
every breath.

Low in the field
wild strawberries
fatten.

Come soon.

It's a matter of
life.

And death.

DRY SPELL

Again,
sunfire in a
cloudless sky.

Another
dry
day.

Hot wind licks
the land,
licking the green away.

Grass cringes,
singes and
dies.

The tree rations water,
the leaf
dries

snaps
falls.

In the brook bed
rocks whiten,
cracks vein the earth.

Roots have forgotten
the taste
of rain.

HAY SONG

The mower's in the meadow
scissoring grass,
tall tufted timothy
redtop and
rye,
              (now let it lie)

felling alfalfa
clipping the clover,
bee, move over!
              (let it dry)

scattering thistle
      in puffs
      of seed
smartweed
sneezeweed
daisy and
yarrow.

Pray
no rain tomorrow.
Let there be

hay,
meadow lunch
for a horse to munch
on a winter day.

SUN DAY

It's a sun day
all faces
lift and
turn.

A sunflower
seven feet tall
raises its
seedheavy head
and quenches a deep
sun thirst.

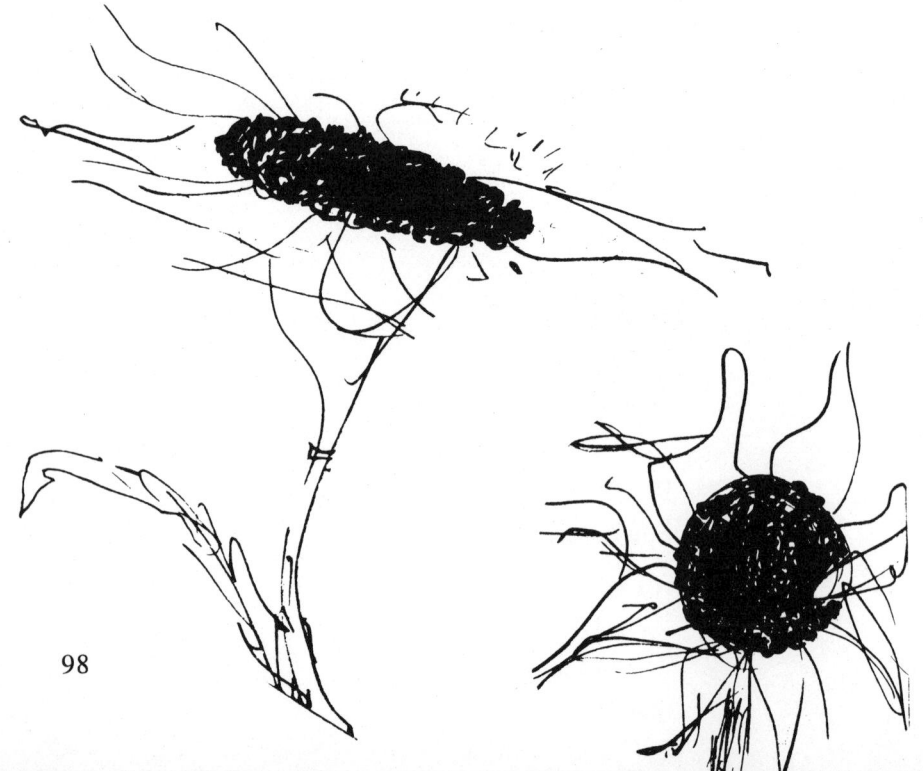

Purplebrown pansies
look up
to ponder
with old men's faces
the wonder
of this
light.

Pale people
in sunglasses
who go home
tomorrow
lie motionless,
borrowing
sun.

All faces
lifting
turning
sun-yearning.

ECOLOGY
(*For George Ember*)

the sturdy clever muskrat
tunneling
the grassy banks
of the pond,
heaping
the rushes and reeds,
gnawing
the sweet and rampant
waterweeds,

the webfooted swimmer
in the bright
water,
eluding the farmer who
hates
earth holes
the trapper who
waits
for a skin —

well, he's gone now

and
the pond is
choking
on
its own wild
grass.

SUNSET

There's dazzle
      in the western sky,
colors spill and
      run.
The pond mouth
lies open
      greedy
for the last drop
of
melting
sun.

ARSON

Slowly
in the long hot days
Virginia creeper
reaches out and
roots and
winds
around a tree.

Reaches,
roots
and
winds
till even dead tree trunks
wear summer green.

A late
September day
the creeper
turns, erupts
to sudden red,
ignites
each captive tree
in ivy flame,
and sets the fires
of autumn
burning
in these hills.

THE CHESTNUTS ARE FALLING

First
the leaf
new and shiny,

then
the catkin's yellow
fur,

then the tiny
bud.

Now
the spiky swelling
burr,
splitting
spilling redbrown satin.

Thud!

SQUIRREL

The squirrel in the hickory tree's a
nervous fellow,
all quiver and scurry.
See him

hurl himself upon
a limb
worry a nut
pack his cheeks
race
downtree
to a secret place and
hurry
back
in furry frenzy.

There's something he knows
that makes him
go,
this soft slow
mellow
autumn day.

It has to do with
hunger
in the snow.

SEPTEMBER

Something is bleeding
into the
pond,
the stains are freshly
red.

Look —
beyond
and overhead.
The maple

is crimson spattered.
Summer is fatally
wounded.
Soon, soon
dead.

RECYCLED

Plank
by plank and
beam
by beam
they opened up the barn,

unsealed
each solid seam,
revealed
its corners to the sky,
and took its wood.

Wood
with weather in its
grain,
its flanks windrubbed and
stained by
rain
and holding deep the pungency
of cow and
hay.

Beam
on beam and
plank
on plank and
miles away,
the barn wood rose, and
closed
around a home.

This sheltering wood is
not yet
done
with ice,
with sun.

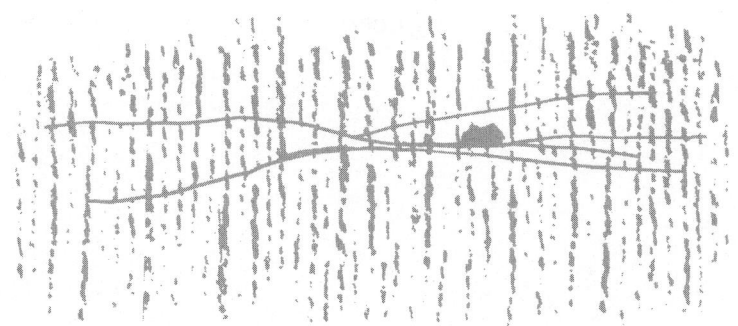

FLIGHT

A hound sound
comes out of the sky

and there are the geese,
a ragged string
moving
heart and wing
    into the wind.

Flung back
unraveled
beating forward
re-knit
    in arrow flight

onward
without choice
to open water
from winter night.

WILLOW YELLOW

The reds of fall
are burned
away

the oaks
are
gray

but the willow's yellow.

Yellow
willow!

Black maples
grow
in new snow
meadows

but the brassy boughs are willow.

Yellow
willow!

WINTER CARDINAL

Fat
and elegantly
crested,
clinging to the branch
of the stripped tree
like
one bright leaf that
bested
every wind and lived
to show
its red
against
the astonished snow.

WEATHER REPORT

Pinging rain
stinging sleet
tonight.

Frost at dawn,
bright
sun in the
morning.

Ice-bearing trees,
a glass
orchard,
blinking
sunwinking.

A noonwind will
pass,
harvesting the brittle crop,
crashing
clinking.

Index of first lines

A bridge   27
A ghostly snow   28
A hound sound   108
A jet screams and climbs   13
A monster   80
Again,   96
All day   5
All night   20

Big   42
Breathe and blow   58

Come soon.   94
Crow knows   75

Dark clouds   12
Don't shake this   41
Ducklings   93

Fat   110
First   103
Fling   35

Giraffe's   79
Go wind, blow   55

Here come the   8
Hey! Cackle! Hey!   63
How did you get here   44

I left my head   66
I like   43

I made a sand castle   54
"I wish,"   65
In the witch's   68
It's a sun day   98
I've seen   28

Listen to a cornstalk   18
Look at that!   67
Look at us!   81
LOST: 70

Moon,   83
mud   49

New sounds to   45
No one at Sam's place   72

Old Witch Winter   23
Older than   21
On this street   33

Pigeons are city folk   30
Pinging rain   111
Plank   106

Sit   59
Slowly   107
Small sounds   46
Someone   14
Something is bleeding   105
Spider's   48
Stand still   58
Strange shadows out   85

"Tell me a story,"   69
That was   47
The children   78
The foghorn moaned   34
The giant mouth   31
The mower's in the meadow   97
The reds of fall   109
The rain   34
The road   10
The shadow of a   84
The sky is   37
The squirrel in the hickory tree's a   104
the sturdy clever muskrat   100
The sun is out   4
The wind   9
There is nothing   32
There's dazzle   101
Thin streams   89
This is the Bridge   64
This is the wind's doing   76
Time ticks,   82

Until I saw the sea   53

Wake   29
We both stood   90
Wet wet wet   91
What happened in the sky   16
When   57
When the wind blows   56
When these small   3
When you've   77
When we've emptied   6
White picket fence   76
Winter dark comes early   36